9-61

DRAW
50 CREEPY
CRAWLIES

Draw 50 Airplanes, Aircraft, and Spacecraft
Draw 50 Aliens, UFOs, Galaxy Ghouls, Milky Way Marauders, and Other
           Extraterrestrial Creatures
Draw 50 Animal 'Toons
Draw 50 Animals
Draw 50 Athletes
Draw 50 Beasties and Yugglies and Turnover Uglies and Things That Go Bump
           in the Night
Draw 50 Birds
Draw 50 Boats, Ships, Trucks, and Trains
Draw 50 Buildings and Other Structures
Draw 50 Cars, Trucks, and Motorcycles
Draw 50 Cats
Draw 50 Creepy Crawlies
Draw 50 Dinosaurs and Other Prehistoric Animals
Draw 50 Dogs
Draw 50 Endangered Animals
Draw 50 Famous Caricatures
Draw 50 Famous Cartoons
Draw 50 Famous Faces
Draw 50 Flowers, Trees, and Other Plants
Draw 50 Holiday Decorations
Draw 50 Horses
Draw 50 Monsters, Creeps, Superheroes, Demons, Dragons, Nerds, Dirts,
           Ghouls, Giants, Vampires, Zombies, and Other Curiosa . . .
Draw 50 People
Draw 50 People of the Bible
Draw 50 Sharks, Whales, and Other Sea Creatures
Draw 50 Vehicles

DRAW 50 CREEPY CRAWLIES

LEE J. AMES
with
RAY BURNS

BROADWAY BOOKS

New York

BROADWAY

Published by Broadway Books
a division of Random House, Inc.
1540 Broadway, New York, New York 10036

BROADWAY BOOKS and its logo, a letter B bisected on the diagonal, are
trademarks of Broadway Books, a division of Random House, Inc.

Library of Congress Cataloging-in-Publication Data

Ames, Lee J.
Draw 50 creepy crawlies/Lee J. Ames with Ray Burns.—1st ed.
p.   cm.
Summary: Step-by-step instructions for drawing fifty different insects, spiders, and
other crawling or flying creatures.
1. Insects in art—Juvenile literature. 2. Animals in art—Juvenile literature. 3.
Drawing—Technique—Juvenile literature. [1. Insects in art. 2. Animals in art. 3.
Drawing—Technique.] I. Burns, Raymond, 1924– . II. Title. III. Title: Draw fifty
creepy crawlies.
NC783.A44   1991
743'.6—dc20   90-19396   CIP   AC

ISBN 0-385-41189-8 (HC)
ISBN 0-385-42449-3 (PB)

SEPTEMBER 1992
FIRST PAPERBACK EDITION

20 19 18 17 16 15 14 13

Thanks again, Ray,
for sharing with me your wonderful talent.
—L.J.A.

To Lee Ames,
a good friend these many years.
—R.B.

TO THE READER

This is number twenty in our "Draw 50" series. This is the twentieth time I've had the fun and privilege of showing you a way of creating drawings. This time it's the method used by Ray Burns and myself. Working with Ray, and bringing his unique talent to the book, made this a most delightful experience.

Ray is a top illustrator of our time. In your library and bookstore, you will find many books that have been enhanced by his talent. In black and white, in full color, from cartoons to fantasy to realism, from fairy tales to history to natural science, he has shown himself to be an expert. Thank you, Ray, for joining with me in this project!

When you start working, I would recommend you use clean white bond paper or drawing paper and a pencil with moderately soft lead (HB or No. 2). Keep a kneaded eraser (available at art supply stores) handy. Choose the creepy crawly you want to draw and then, very lightly and very carefully, sketch out the first step. Also very lightly and carefully, add the second step. As you go along, study not only the lines but the spaces between the lines. Size your first steps as closely as possible to the lines and the spaces in the book—not too large, not too small. Remember, the first steps must be constructed with the greatest care. A mistake here could ruin the entire drawing.

As you work, it's a good idea to hold a mirror to your sketch from time to time. The image in the mirror frequently shows distortion you might not have noticed otherwise.

In the book, new steps are printed darker than the previous steps. This is so they can be clearly seen. But you should keep your construction steps very light. Here's where the kneaded eraser can be useful. You can use it to lighten a pencil stroke that is too dark.

When you've completed all the steps, and when you're sure you have everything the way you want it, complete the drawing with firm, strong penciling. If you like, you can go over this with India ink (applied with a fine brush or pen), or a permanent fine-tipped ballpoint or felt-tipped marker. When your work is thoroughly dry, you can then use the kneaded eraser to clean out all the underlying pencil marks.

Always remember that even if your first attempts at drawing do not turn out the way you'd like, it's important to *keep trying.* Your efforts *will* eventually pay off and you'll be pleased by what you can accomplish.

I sincerely hope you will improve your drawing skills and have a great time working on these creepers and crawlers.

LEE J. AMES

TO THE PARENT OR TEACHER

In fourth grade, many years ago, we were given an assignment to draw something to honor President Lincoln's birthday. An immediate competition developed among the four or five class artists. Which of us could draw the best portrait of Honest Abe?

We, of course, would not agree that any other one of us did the best. Our pride led each of us to consider himself the winner. Today I couldn't honestly make the judgment call that mine deserved to be number one, but I did learn something that ultimately resulted in the "Draw 50" books.

I learned the importance of peer approval. The encouragement given to us artists by the rest of the class and the praise we gave one another was heady inspiration. Most of the group went on to become successful professionals.

All the drawings of Abraham Lincoln that the class artists made were copied from other sources. This despite general disapproval of "copying." We copied from the Lincoln penny; from a five-dollar bill; from a calendar; and from sale advertisements in the newspaper. We copied someone else's work, stroke by stroke, and we erased and reworked. Many considered this to be a noncreative, harmful way to learn drawing. But we liked what we finally got. Our friends and classmates liked what we did and we were encouraged. We were on a roll, and that was of overriding importance.

Later we were able to learn technique, theory, media, and much more with the gift of incentive provided by friends, classmates, and family. Early on we copied, then we found ways to do our own original things.

Mimicry is prerequisite to creativity!

It is my hope that my readers will be able to come up with drawings that will bring them gratifying approval from friends, classmates, and family. After that I look forward to the competition.

Enjoy!

LEE J. AMES

DRAW
50 CREEPY
CRAWLIES

Firefly

Bumblebee

European Corn Borer Moth

Winged Termite

Unicorn Beetle

Assassin Bug

Walking Stick

Predacious Diving Beetle

Springtail

Bald-Faced Hornet

Housefly

American Cockroach

Army Worm

Bedbug

Scorpion Fly

Head Louse

Horntail

Dung Beetle

Buffalo Treehopper

Black Widow Spider

Tarantula

Wolf Spider

Slug

Snail

Scorpion

Millipede

Centipede

Caterpillar

Back Swimmer

Field Cricket

Cicada

Water Strider